THE HOI

THE ANCIENT PROVINCE OF TUSAYAN.

BY MAJOR J. W. POWELL.

MOQUI PUEBLO.

FILTER PRESS

Palmer Lake, Colorado

1972

FILTER PRESS
Wild and Woolly West Books
Phone (303) 481-2523

P.O. Box 5, Palmer Lake, Colorado 80133

1. Choda — Thirty Pound Rails, 1956
2. Clemens — Celebrated Jumping Frog, 1965
3. Banks — Uncle Jim's Book of Pancakes, 1967, 1979.
4. Service — Yukon Poems, 1967
5. Cushing — My Adventures In Zuni, 1967
6. Englert — Oliver Perry Wiggins, 1968 *(Out of Print)*
7. Matthews — Navajo Weavers & Silversmiths, 1968
8. Campbell — Wet Plates & Dry Gulches, 1970
9. Banks — Alferd Packer's Wilderness Cookbook, 1969
10. Faulk — Simple Methods of Mining Gold, 1969
11. Rusho — Powell's Canyon Voyage, 1969
12. Hinckley — Transcontinental Rails, 1969
13. Young — The Grand Canyon, 1969
14. Gehm — Nevada's Yesterdays, 1970 *(Out of Print)*
15. Seig — Tobacco, Peace Pipes, & Indians, 1971
16. Conrotto — Game Cookery Recipes, 1971 *(Out of Print)*
17. Scanland — Life of Pat F. Garrett, 1971
18. Hunt — High Country Ghost Town Poems, 1962, 1971
19. Arpad — Buffalo Bill's Wild West, 1971
20. Wheeler — Deadwood Dick's Leadville Lay, 1971 *(Out of Print)*
21. Powell — The Hopi Villages, 1972
22. Bathke — The West in Postage Stamps, 1973 *(Out of Print)*
23. Hesse — Southwestern Indian Recipe Book, 1973
24. Vangen — Indian Weapons, 1972 *(Out of Print)*
25. MacDonald — Cockeyed Charley Parkhurst, 1973
26. Schwatka — Among the Apaches, 1974
27. Bourke — General Crook in the Indian Country *and*
    Remington — A Scout with the Buffalo Soldiers, 1974
28. Powell — An Overland Trip to the Grand Canyon, 1974
29. Harte — Luck of Roaring Camp & other sketches, 1975
30. Remington — On The Apache Reservations & Among the Cheyennes, 1974
31. Ferrin — Many Moons Ago, 1976 *(Out of Print)*
32. Kirby — Saga of Butch Cassidy, 1977 *(Out of Print)*
33. Isom — Fox Grapes, Cherokee Verse, 1977 *(Out of Print)*
34. Bryan — Navajo Native Dyes, 1978
35. deBaca — Vicente Silva, Terror of Las Vegas, 1978
36. Underhill — Pueblo Crafts, 1979
37. Underhill — Papago & Pima Indians of Arizona, 1979
38. Riker — Colorado Ghost Towns & Mining Camps, 1979
39. Bennett — Genuine Navajo Rug: How to Tell, 1979
40. Duran — Blonde Chicana Bride's Mexican Cookbook, 1980
41. Kennard — Field Mouse Goes to War, 1977
42. Keasey — Gadsden's Silent Observers, 1974
43. Beshoar — Violet Soup, 1982
44. Underhill — People of the Crimson Evening, 1982
45. Choda — The West on Wood, 5. Vols, *(In preparation)*
46. Duran — Mexican Recipe Shortcuts, 1983
47. Roosevelt — In Cowboy Land, *(In preparation)*

ISBN 0-910584-28-1 cloth
ISBN 0-910584-73-7 paper
L.C.#75-25049

THE NAMES OF THE HOPI TOWNS

The modern names are shown first, followed by older forms.

First Mesa (The Moqui Towns)
    Hano or Tewa. Settled by Tewa Indians from the Rio Grande. Some say
        the name Hano came from the Tewa habit of saying, "hah?"
    Sichomovi or Sichoamavi, the middle village.
    Walpi or Wolpi, the "Place of the Notch" on extreme end of the mesa

Second Mesa
    Mishongnovi or Mishonginivi
    Shipaulovi or Shipauiluvi
    Shongopovi or Shongapavi, also called Shumapovi

Third Mesa
    Oraibi
    New villages are Hotevilla, Bakabi, and New Oraibi

Moenkopi, near Tuba City, was founded by people from Old Oraibi.
    Originally merely a seasonal farming community, it is now occupied year
    round by some families, although they return to Oraibi for ceremonies.

You may have noted that your copy of **ARIZONA, A STATE GUIDE** spells
two town names as Sichomoir and Shipoloir. This misprint was begun in
1940, and apparently is preserved for all future generations. It began from an
error in copying handwritten notes.

The Ancient Village of Walpi

INTRODUCTION

As we drove up the steep, narrow road along the cliff to the top of First Mesa, on our first visit to the Hopi villages of Hano, Sichomovi, and Walpi, we could almost feel we were going up to the "Second story of the World." This was where the "good People" had been brought by Machita to make the beginning of our world in which we live. We drove up and up to reach these villages which are on a narrow mesa far above the surrounding land. Although they have, of course, changed through the years they are still much the same as when Major John Wesley Powell visited them.

Hopi terrace oven, Walpi

There are many more houses now, but they still follow the same pattern and many of the old ones remain unchanged. Now there are automobiles parked in front of the houses, power lines, television antennae, and a water tank. However, the charm and interest of these villages built so high in the sky, is still the same. We could almost imagine that we were going up with Major Powell.

Our trip to First Mesa was on October 13, 1966. This was almost exactly 96 years after Powell had reached there. He arrived on October 24, 1870, after spending some time in the other Hopi villages to the west.

As we drove up on top we were immediately joined by several enthusiastic, grinning small boys, hoping for the candy bar gifts of the tourist. We supplied these, and were told, "There's a dance on Walpi today." To our question, "Is it all right for us to go?", our friendly guides replied, "Sure, we'll take you." We knew, of course, that a dance at an Indian village usually is a ceremonial, not a social dance. We parked in Sichomovi to walk across the narrow notch of land which gives Walpi its name "place of the notch." This notch is, in reality, a long narrow neck of rock, 10 feet wide, with sides almost perpendicular to the land hundreds of feet below. Walpi itself is barely 150 feet across at its widest point.

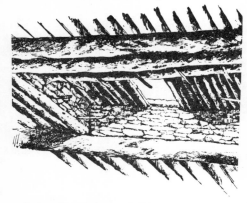

Interior view of Kiva hatchway

It was a cold day with the wind so strong we felt it might blow us over the mesa edge to the land far below. We wondered how these houses could have remained perched there on the edge through the storms of all these years.

The boys happily guided us across, past the entrances to the underground kivas into which they peered with typical small boy curiosity, to a fairly sheltered courtyard near Dance Rock. There we found seats in niches in the walls of surrounding houses. A

friendly Walpi lady made room for me by her and a small boy, her grandson, who was shivering in the cold wind. I put my parka around him too, and we helped keep each other warm. As women will, we began to talk as we waited. We discussed the same subjects that women usually discuss — the high cost of children's clothes, of eyeglasses, and naturally, the weather. "This windstorm," she told me, "is the tail end of that hurricane down south."

Stone steps at Oraibi

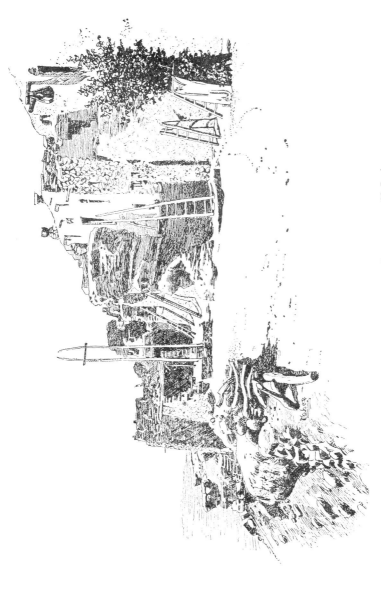

Dance Rock and Dance Court, at Walpi

When the dancers came out of the kiva we were back 96 years in time, watching them with Powell. We forgot the wind, the sandstorm, and the cold. We felt ourselves a part of the whole unreal scene. At the end of the dance, the ladies in the audience ran forward to grab the ears of corn held by the dancers. My friend came back with hers and said to us, "I got the corn. You come back tomorrow and eat

A Chimney Pot

at my house." As we started away one tourist asked us, "Is this all there is?" I turned to him, ashamed of his Anglo ignorance, and asked, "What more could you want?" The Indians disappeared into their homes while those from the other villages started back across the narrow neck of land. The wind had risen so it was almost impossible to walk upright. We felt in real danger now of being blown over the edge. So, too, did some crying children whose mother was trying to take them across. My husband took one baby while I held the hand of another, and together we all struggled across the windy gap to their house where we left them.

Piki stone and chimney hood, at Sichomovi

That day too, we met the friendly Chief of the First Mesa and his wife. Since we wanted to buy some of her pottery we were invited into their home to see it. We bought the pottery; we ladies admired each other's turquoise jewelry while the men discussed the problems of managing villages.

Finally it was time for us to start down from the Mesa. We did not want to leave for we knew we could not return the next day, and we were not ready to go back to our own hurried, confused part of the the world. As we drove down the road in the twilight we felt we had just had a very special day. We had truly been with the "good people" on the Mesa.

SOUTH PASSAGEWAY OF WALPI.

Roof drains, made of old metate and gourd

We have been back to the Hopi villages many times but that was our most memorable visit. We have been there on sunnier days to visit the Chief and his friendly wife and daughter. We have been to the Second Mesa where I met my little friend, then 10 years old, with whom I still correspond. She writes me of her school and of the Kachina dances. At Christmas she sends me gifts from the Hopi mesa, always signing her name, "your friend." As Powell wrote, "These are hospitable and polite people."

If I were writing a dedication of this reprint of Major Powell's article, *The Ancient Province of Tusayan,* it would surely be "To my friends of the Hopi Mesas."

Major Powell's article was written in 1875. We have used additional illustrations of the same period. A large number were taken from Victor Mindeleff's *Study of Pueblo Architecture in Tusayan and Cibola* which appeared in the *Eighth Annual Report of the Bureau of Ethnology.*

Palmer Lake, March 1972   Lollie W. Campbell

Court Kiva of Shongopovi

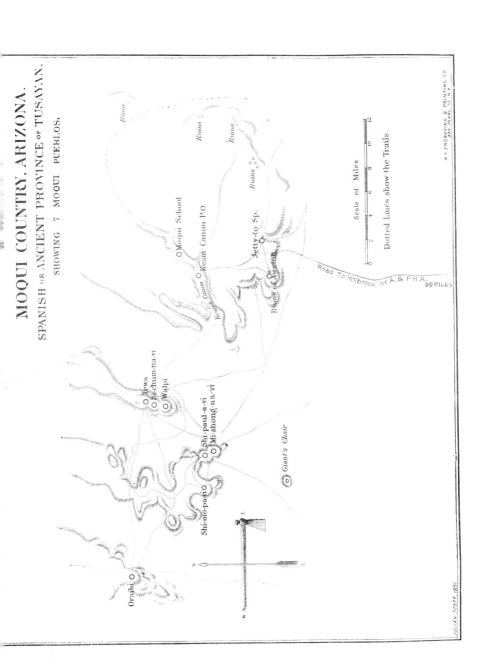

MOQUI COUNTRY, ARIZONA.

SPANISH OR ANCIENT PROVINCE OF TUSAYAN.

SHOWING 7 MOQUI PUEBLOS,

Ruins

Ruins

Ruins

Ruins

Ruins

Moqui School

Keam Canon P.O.

Keam Canon

Jetty-to Sp.

Ruins of Au-wat-ovi

Ruins of Kwai-ki-oo

Road To Holbrook, on A. & P. R. R.

90 MILES

Scale of Miles

Dotted Lines show the Trails.

N. Y. ENGRAVING & PRINTING CO.
320 PEARL ST., N. Y.

Te-wa

Si-chum-na-vi

Walpi

Shi-paul-a-vi

Mi-shong-na-vi

Shi-mo-pa-vi

Giant's Chair

Orabi

JULIAN SCOTT, 1891

John Wesley Powell

THE HOPI VILLAGES:

THE ANCIENT PROVINCE OF TUSAYAN.

BY MAJOR J. W. POWELL.

WOL-PI, A VILLAGE IN THE TUSAYAN COUNTRY.

It was the 23d of September. We had made an overland trip from Salt Lake City to the Grand Cañon of the Colorado,* and were now on the bank of the Kanab, on the way back to the rendezvous camp at the upper springs of the river, which was yet about forty miles away, and which was to be our point of departure for the "Province of Tusayan."

Since the exploration was made of which

* See SCRIBNER'S MONTHLY for October, 1875.
VOL. XI.—13.

---

* John Wesley Powell, one-armed veteran of the Civil War, had led an expedition down the unknown canyons of the Colorado River. Jacob Hamblin was sent by Brigham Young to await them at the end of the voyage. Hamblin later helped Powell learn the fate of two deserters from his exploration party. The two new friends, one Mormon, the other Methodist, then made an overland trip to the Hopi-land described here. Powell continued his explorations, and became director of the U.S. Geological Survey, and of the Bureau of Ethnology.

I am giving a general account in these papers, this stream has been carefully surveyed. Let me describe it. It is about eighty miles long, and in its course runs through three cañons, which we have called the upper, middle, and lower Kanab cañons. Along its upper course for about a dozen miles it is a permanent stream, but just before entering the first cañon the water is lost in the sands. It is only in seasons of extreme rains that the water flows through this cañon, which is dry sometimes for two or three years in succession. The bed of the stream is usually dry between the upper and middle cañon. At the head of the middle cañon the water again gushes out in springs, and there is a continual stream for a dozen miles. About five miles below this cañon the water again sinks in the sands, and for ten miles or more the stream is lost, except in times of great rains, as above. This usually dry course of the stream is along a level plain where the sands drift, and sometimes obliterate all traces of the water-course. At the head of the lower cañon springs are again found, and the waters gather so as to form, in most seasons, a pretty little creek, though, in seasons of extreme drought, this is dry nearly down to the Colorado; but, in seasons of great rains, immense torrents roll down the gorge. Thus we have a curiously interrupted creek. In three parts of its course it is a permanent stream, and in two parts intermittent.

The point where we struck the Kanab was at the foot of the middle cañon, where the flow of waters is perpetual, and just there we found a few pioneers of a Mormon town, to be called, after the stream, Kanab. At that time these people were living in what they called a "fort"—that is, several little cabins had been built about a square, the doors and windows opening toward the plaza, the backs of their houses connected by a rude stockade made of cedar poles planted on end. This "fort" was intended for defense against the Indians.

The way in which these Mormon settlements are planted is very interesting. The authorities of the "Church of Jesus Christ of Latter-Day Saints" determine to push a settlement into a new region. The country is first explored and the site for a town selected, for all settlements are made by towns. The site having been chosen, it is surveyed and divided into small lots of about an acre, with outlying lots of five or ten acres. Then a number of people are

selected "to go on mission," as it is termed. The list is made out in this way : The President of the Church, with his principal bishops and other officers, meet in consultation, and select from the various settlements throughout the territory persons whom they think it would be well to send to the new place. Many are the considerations entering into this selection. First, it is necessary to have an efficient business man, one loyal to the Church, as bishop or ruler of the place, and he must have certain counselors ; it is necessary, too, that the various trades shall be represented in the village—they want a blacksmith, shoemaker, etc. Again, in making the selection, it is sometimes thought wise to take men who are not working harmoniously with the authorities where they are residing ; and thus they have a thorough discussion of the various parties, and the reasons why they are needed here and there ; but at last the list is made out. The President of the Church then presents these names to the General Conference of the Church for its approval, and that body having confirmed the nominations (and perhaps there is no instance known where a nomination is not confirmed), the people thus selected are notified that at a certain time they are expected "to go on a mission" to establish a new town. Sometimes a person selected, feeling aggrieved with the decision of the Church, presents his reasons to the President for wishing to remain, and occasionally such a person is excused, but the reasons must be very urgent. So far as my observation goes, there is rarely any determined opposition to the decision of the Conference.

So the people move to their new home. Usually there are four lots in a square, and four persons unite to fence the same, each receiving a garden. The out-lots are fenced as one great farm. The men, living in covered wagons or tents, or having built cabins or other shelter for themselves, set to work under the bishop or one of his subordinates to fence the farm, and make the canals and minor water-ways necessary to the irrigation of the land. The water-ditch and fence of the farm are common property. As soon as possible a little store is established, all of the principal men of the community taking stock in it, usually aided more or less by "Zion's Coöperative Mercantile Institution," the great wholesale establishment in Salt Lake City. In the same way saw-mills and grist-mills are built.

Such is a brief outline of the establish-

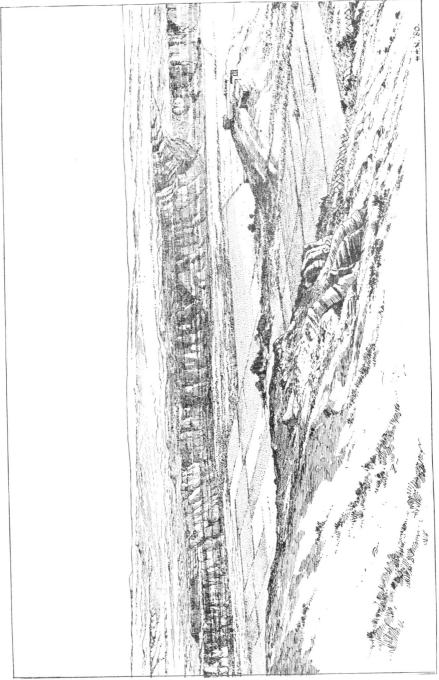

THE SITE OF MOEN-KOPI.

3

Paneled wooden doors at Hano

4

ment of a Mormon town; in like manner, all of the towns throughout the territory of Utah have branched out from the original trunk at Salt Lake City, so that they are woven together by a net-work of communal interest.

The missionary, Jacob Hamblin, who was traveling with us, came here two or three years ago and established himself in a little cabin, about which during the greater part of each season a few Indians were gathered. When we came to the place, we found the men at work cutting and hauling hay, while a number of squalid Indians were lounging in the "fort," and many children of white and Indian breed were playing in the meadow. Such a community is a strange medley of humanity. There are no physicians here, but the laying on of hands by the elders is frequently practiced, and every old man and woman of the community has some wonderful cure—a relic of ancient sorcery. Almost every town has its astrologer, and every family one or more members who see visions and dream dreams. Aged and venerable men, with solemn ceremony, are endowed by the Church with the power of prophecy and the gift of blessing. So the grandfather recounts the miracles which have been performed by the prophets; the grandmother tells of the little beast that has its nest in the heart, and when it wanders around toward the lungs causes consumption; the mother dreams dreams; the daughter consults the astrologer, and the son seeks for a sign in the heavens. At every gathering for preaching on a Sunday morning, or dancing on a weekday night, a prayer is offered. When they gather at table, thanks are rendered to the Giver of Bounties, and on all occasions, and in the most earnest manner, when a stranger is met, the subject of miracles, the persecution of the saints, and the virtue and wisdom of polygamy are discussed.

ALCOVE BAD LANDS

Good roads are built to every settlement, at great expense and with much labor. The best agricultural implements are found on the farms, and the telegraph clicks in every village.

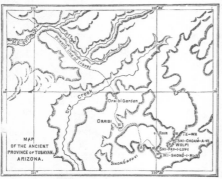

Altogether, a Mormon town is a strange mixture of Oriental philosophy and morals, primitive superstitions and modern inventions.

I must not fail to mention here the kind treatment which I have almost invariably received from the people living in the frontier settlements of Southern Utah.

At Kanab, the party divided, Mr. Hamblin, with one man, going to Tokerville—a settlement about fifty miles to the northwest—for the purpose of procuring some additional supplies. With the remainder of the party I proceeded up the Kanab. The trail was very difficult; it was impossible to climb the cliffs and go over the plateau with our animals, and we had to make our way up the cañon. In many places the stream runs over beds of quicksand, sweeping back and forth in short curves from wall to wall, so that we were compelled to ford it now and then; again, there is a dense undergrowth, and, at many places, the stream is choked with huge bowlders which have fallen from the cliffs. The plateau, or terrace, through which this cañon is cut, slopes backward to the north, and, by ascending the stream, we at last reached its summit, and found it covered with a sea of drifting sands, golden and vermilion; so we named it Sand-Dune Plateau. Just before us, there was another line of cliffs—a great wall of shining white sandstone, a thousand feet high.

We soon entered another cañon, but this was dry. At some very late geological period a stream of lava has rolled down it, so that we had to pass over beds of black clanking basalt. At night, having emerged from the upper cañon, we found the Kanab a living stream once more, and camped upon its bank.

The next day we passed up the beautiful valley for ten miles, and arrived at the rendezvous camp. Here I was to wait for a few days for Mr. Hamblin's arrival. I kept the Indians and one white man with me, and Mr. Nebeker, with the remainder of the party and a single Indian guide, started for the Colorado River, at the mouth of the Paria, by a well traveled Indian trail. We had brought a quantity of lumber to this point with wagons, for the purpose of building a ferry-boat on the Colorado. These boards were cut into short pieces and packed on mules, and Mr. Nebeker was to push on to the river, construct the boat, get the train across, and have everything in readiness, on the opposite side of the river, by the time of our arrival. My purpose was to demonstrate the practicability of this route to the river, then to cross at the mouth of the Paria, and proceed thence to the "Province of Tusayan," in north-eastern Arizona.

The Indians we had with us were not acquainted with the country beyond the

ASH-TISH-KEL, A CHIEF OF THE NAVAJOS.

river, and it was necessary to obtain some new aids, so I sent Chu-ar to the Kaibab Plateau, a hundred miles to the south-east, with instructions to collect the Indians who inhabit that region at a designated spring, and hold them until my arrival.

I waited a week in the upper valley of

6

the Kanab, the time being chiefly spent in talking with the Indians, and trying to learn something of their language. By day the men hunted, and the women gathered berries and the other rich fruits that grow in that country, and at night they danced. A little after dark a fire was kindled, and the musicians took their places. They had two kinds of instruments. One was a large basket tray, covered with pitch inside and out, so as to be quite hard and resonant; this was placed over a pit in the ground,

Gradually they formed a circle, and the dance commenced. Around they went, old men and women, young men and maidens, little boys and girls, in one great circle, around and around, all singing, all keeping time with their feet, pat, pat, pat, in the dust and sand; low, hoarse voices; high, broken, screaming voices; mellow, tender voices; but louder than all, the thump and screech of the orchestra.

One set done, another was formed; this time the women dancing in the inner circle,

THE THOUSAND WELLS.

and they beat on it with sticks. The other was a primitive fiddle, made of a cedar stick, as large around as my wrist and about three feet long; this was cut with notches about three inches apart. They placed one end on a tray arranged like the one just described, placed the other end against the stomach, and played upon the fiddle with a pine-stick bow, which was dragged up and down across the notches, making a rattling, shrieking sound. So they beat their loud drum and sawed their hoarse fiddle for a time, until the young men and maidens gathered about and joined in a song:

"Ki-ap-pa tú-gu-wun,
Pí-vi-an-na kaí -va."

(Friends, let the play commence;
All sing together.)

the men without. Then they formed in rows, and danced, back and forth, in lines. the men in one direction, the women in another. Then they formed again, the men standing expectant without, the women dancing demurely within, quite independent of one another, until one maiden beckoned to a lover, and he, with a loud, shrill whoop, joined her in the sport. The ice broken, each woman called for her partner; and so they danced by twos and twos, in and out, here and there, with steadily increasing time, until one after another broke down and but three couples were left. These danced on, on, on, until they seemed to be wild with uncontrollable motion. At last one of the couples failed, and the remaining two pattered away, while the whole tribe stood by shouting, yelling, laughing, and screaming, until another couple broke down, and the champions only remained. Then all the people rushed forward, and the winning couple were carried and pushed by the crowd to the fire. The and went up a gulch, where we hoped to find water in a limestone pocket, but were disappointed. This compelled us to continue our journey long into the night. The direction traveled was now to the south, and our way was up a long cañon valley, with

INTERIOR OF ORAIBI HOUSE.

old chief came up, and on the young man's head placed a crown of eagle feathers. A circlet of braided porcupine quills was placed about the head of the maiden, and into this circlet were inserted plumes made of the crest of the quail and the bright feathers of the humming-bird.

On the first of October, Mr. Hamblin having returned from Tokerville, we started for the Kaibab Plateau to meet the Indians, as had been arranged with Chu-ar. That night we camped in the cañon of the Skoom-pa. This is really a broad cañon valley, the walls of which are of red sandstone. On the lower reaches of these walls, near some springs, there are many hieroglyphics, some of them so high up as to be beyond reach, in the present condition of the talus at the foot of the cliffs.

The next day our course was through barren sage plains until, about four o'clock, we came to the foot of the Kaibab Plateau,

high mountains on either side. At last we reached a spring, and camped.

Three hours' travel the next morning brought us to the spring at which we were to meet the Indians, but none were seen. High up on the mountain to the east was a signal smoke, which we understood, by previous arrangement, meant that we were to cross the Kaibab Plateau. We staid in camp the remainder of that day to rest.

The next day we started early, climbing to the summit of the plateau, more than two thousand feet up a long, rocky gulch; then through a forest of giant pines, with glades here and there, and now and then a lake. Occasionally a herd of deer was started. In this upper region, eight thousand feet above the level of the sea, even the clouds of northern Arizona yield moisture sufficient for forest growth and rich meadows. At dusk we descended from the plateau

A KIVA HATCHWAY OF TUSAYAN.

HHN '90.

9

on the eastern side, found a spring at its foot, and camped.

The next day we crossed a broad valley to the foot of the line of Vermilion Cliffs, and at two o'clock reached the designated spring, where we found our Indians. They had already arranged that Na-pu and To-ko-puts (Old Man and Wild Cat) should be our guides from the Colorado River to the "Province of Tusayan."

During the evening I was very much interested in obtaining from them a census of their little tribe. They divided the arithmetic into parts, each of four men taking a certain number of families. Each sat down and counted on his fingers and toes the persons belonging to the families allotted to him, going over them again and again until each finger and toe stood in his mind for an individual. Then he would discuss the matter with other Indians, to see that all were enumerated, something like this : " Did you count Jack ? " " Yes ; that finger stands for Jack." " Did you count Nancy ? " " Yes ; that toe is Nancy." Each of the census takers becoming satisfied that he had correctly enumerated his portion, he procured the number of sticks necessary to represent them, and gave them to me. Adding the four together, I had the census of the tribe —seventy-three. Then I set them to dividing them severally into groups of men, women and children, but this I found a hard task. They could never agree among themselves whether certain persons should be called children, or not ; but, at last, I succeeded in obtaining the number of males and females.

The next morning I distributed some presents of knives, tobacco, beads, and other trinkets, and we pushed on toward the Colorado River. We found a difficult trail, having to cross the heads of many abrupt, but not very deep cañons. Down and up we climbed all day long, winding about here and there, and always among the rocks, until at night we joined our party at the mouth of the Paria, and were ferried over to their camp.

Early the next morning I climbed the Vermilion Cliffs. This great escarpment or wall of flaring red rock in a general direction faces south, from Saint George on the Rio Virgen to a point many miles east of the Colorado River, a distance of more than three hundred miles as we follow the meandering line. There is a deep re-entrant angle at the mouth of the Paria, where I climbed. Standing on an elevated point on the cliffs, and looking southward, I could see over a stretch of country that steadily rose in the distance until it reached an altitude far above even the elevated point of observation ; and then, meandering through it to the south, the gorge in which the river runs, everywhere breaking down with a sharp brink, and the summits of the walls appearing to approach until they merged in a black line ; and could hardly resist the thought that the river burrowed into, and was lost in, the great inclined plateau. This gorge was Marble Cañon, described in a previous article.

While I was climbing, the train pushed on, in a direction a little to the east of south, along the foot of the Vermilion Cliffs. By mid-afternoon I overtook it. The trail by which we were traveling led up into a deep gulch, and we came to a clear, beautiful spring, gushing from beneath a rock a thousand feet high. Here was indeed "the shadow of a great rock in a weary land," and here we camped for the night. All about us were evidences of an ancient town or hamlet, foundation walls of houses half buried in débris, fragments of pottery painted with rude devices, and picture writings etched on the cliffs.

For another day, our journey was at the foot of the Vermilion Cliffs, in a direction a little east of south, over naked hills of sand and marls, where we found briny springs occasionally, but no fresh water, and no grass ; a desert, but a painted desert ; not a desert plain, but a desert of hills, and cliffs, and rocks—a region of alcove lands. At night we found a little water, in a basin or pocket, a mile from the trail.

The next day we went to the top of the *mesa* by climbing the cliffs, and found a billowy sea of sand-dunes. The line of cliffs, separating the mesa above from the deeply gulch-carved plain below, is a long irregular and ragged region, higher by many hundred feet than the general surface of the mesa itself. On the slope of this ridge, facing the mesa, there is a massive, homogeneous sandstone, and the waters, gathering on the brink of the ridge and rolling down this slope, have carved innumerable channels ; and, as they tumble down precipitously in many places, they dig out deep pot-holes, many of them holding a hundred or a thousand barrels of water. Among these holes we camped, finding a little bunch grass among the sand-dunes for our animals. We called this spot the Thousand Wells.

Leaving the wells, we trudged for a day among the sand-dunes, and at night found

A TUSAYAN INTERIOR.

O-RAI-BI

SHI-MO-PA-VI

MI-SHONG-NA-V

SHI-PAUL-A-VI

JULIAN SCOTT, 1891.

7 MOQUI
APACH
SPANISH OR AN

12

WALPI

SI-CHUM-NA-VI TEWA

AGES OR PUEBLOS

NTY ARIZONA

"PROVINCE OF TUSAYAN."

a deep cave in a ledge of rocks, and, in the farther end of the cave, a beautiful lake. Here our Indian guides discovered evidences that led them to believe that our track was followed by some prowling Indians. In the sands about the cave were human tracks; these our guides studied for some time, and, while they were thus engaged, the white men of the party also

A NAVAJO BOY.

talked the matter over, with a little anxiety, for we were now in the country of the Navajos, who had lately been making raids on the Mormon settlements, stealing horses and cattle, and occasionally killing a man, and we feared that they might be following us.

In talking with Na-pu, he assured me that they were not Navajos, but doubtless belonged to a band of Indians known to our tribe as Kwai-an-ti-kwok-ets, or "Beyond the river people," and were their friends. His reasons were these: The tracks which they made in the sand were evidently made with moccasins having projecting soles, like those worn by our Indians and their friends, while the moccasins worn by the Navajos have no such projecting soles. Again, one of the tracks, as he showed me, was made by a lame man, with his right leg shortened, so that he could only walk on the toes of that foot, and this, he said, was the case with the chief of the Kwai-an-ti-kwok-ets. Again, said Na-pu, they would not have walked in places where their tracks would be exposed had they been unfriendly. The conclusion he came to was that they were anxious to see us, but were afraid we had hostile intentions. I directed him to go to an eminence near by and kindle a signal-fire. This he did, and, an hour afterward, three Indians came up. We sat and talked with them until midnight; but they seemed surly fellows, and the conversation was not satisfactory to me. At last they left us; but, for fear they would attempt to steal some of our animals, I had the latter collected, and, finding that we should lose our rest by watching them, I concluded that we might as well continue our journey. So, at two o'clock, everything was packed, we took breakfast, and started, finding our way across the country in the direction we wished to travel, guided by the stars.

Na-pu, the old Indian guide, usually rode with me, while To-ko-puts remained with the men who were managing the pack train. The old man was always solemn and quite reticent, but that day I noticed that he was particularly surly. At last I asked him why. "Why you never call me 'a brick'?" he replied. The answer, of course, astonished me; but, on thinking, and talking with him a little further, I understood the matter. For the previous two or three days we had been quite anxious about water, and the other man, To-ko-puts, when camping time came, usually ran ahead after consulting with Na-pu; finding the watering-place, he would kindle a signal-smoke for us to come on. On arriving, the men, pleased with the Indian's success, would call him "a brick," and thus, it seemed to the old man, that the younger took all the honors away from him; and he explained to me that in his boyhood he had lived in this country,

14

and that it was his knowledge that guided To-ko-puts altogether. I soothed his wounded feelings in this way. He could see that To-ko-puts laughed and talked with the "boys," and was a boy with the rest, but that he (Na-pu) and I were old men, and I recognized his wisdom in the matter. This satisfied him, and ever after that he seemed to be at great pains to talk no more with the younger members of the party, but always came to me.

At ten o'clock we came in sight of a deep

and castles are a million lizards: great red and black lizards, the kings of nobles; little gray lizards, the common people, and here and there a priestly rattlesnake.

We went into camp early in the day, and, with Mr. Hamblin, I started away to the north to visit what had often been described to me as an artificial wall extending across the country for many miles, and one, two, or three hundred feet high; it was claimed, further, that the blocks of which the wall was composed had been carried

TERRACED HOUSES IN ORAIBI—SHOWING ENTRANCE TO KIVA IN THE FOREGROUND.

depression made by the Mo-an-ka-pi, a little stream which enters the Colorado Chiquito. Before us, two or three miles, was the meandering creek, with a little fringe of green willows, box-elders, and cotton-woods ; from these, sage plains stretched back to the cliffs that form the walls of the valley. These cliffs are rocks of bright colors, golden, vermilion, purple and azure hues, and so storm-carved as to imitate Gothic and Grecian architecture on a vast scale. Outlying buttes were castles, with minaret and spire; the cliffs, on either side, were cities looking down into the valley, with castles standing between; the inhabitants of these cities

from a great distance, from the fact that they were not rocks found in that region, but only to the north-west, among the mountains. We were well mounted and rode across the country at a good gallop, for nearly a score of miles, when we came to the wonderful wall, the fame of which had spread among all the Mormon towns to the west. We found it in fact to be an igneous dike, the blocks composed of columnar basalt. In the joints between the blocks there is often an accumulation of a whitish mineral, having the effect, in a rude way, of suggesting mortar. It is not, in fact, a single dike, but a number, radiating from a common center, a great mass of basalt, forming quite a large hill, which the Indians call Kwi-pan-chom, a word signifying "axe hill," for here the Indians of the adjacent country obtain the material for their axes.

Late in the evening a number of Navajo Indians rode up to our camp. One of them could speak a little Spanish or Mexican *patois*. After a little conversation, they concluded to stay with us during the night, tempted, perhaps, by the sight and odor of biscuits and coffee. They were fine-looking fellows, tall and lithe, with keen eyes, sharp features, and faces full of animation. After supper, our new friends and the Kai-bab-it guides sat down for a conference. It was very interesting to observe their means of communicating thought to each other. Neither understood the oral language of the other, but they made maps with their fingers in the sand describing the whereabouts of the several tribes, and seemed to have a great deal of general discussion by means of a sign language. Whenever an Indian's tongue is tied he can talk all over; and so they made gestures, struck attitudes, grunted, frowned, laughed, and altogether had a lively time.

The next morning a Navajo boy offered to go with us to Oraibi, for the purpose of showing us the shortest way. After dinner, we descended from the table-land on which we had been riding, into a deep valley, and, having crossed this, commenced to ascend a steep rocky mesa slope by a well-worn trail, and were surprised, on approaching the summit, to find the slope terraced by rude masonry, which had evidently been made with great labor. These terraces, two or three acres in all, were laid out in nice little gardens, carefully irrigated by training water from a great spring in little channels among the garden plats. Here we found a number of men, women and children from the town of Oraibi gathering their vegetables. They received us with hearty welcome and feasted us on melons. Then we pushed on in company with our new-found friends, rather a mixed crowd now—white men, Kai-bab-its, Navajos, and Shi-nu-mos.

A little before sundown we arrived at Oraibi, the principal town in the "Province of Tusayan," and were met by some of the men, who, at our request, informed us where we could find a good camp. Later in the evening, the chief, who was absent when we arrived, came to camp, and placed our animals in charge of two young men, who took them to a distance from the town and herded them for the night.

The "Province of Tusayan" is composed of seven towns—Oraibi, Shi-pau-i-luv-i, Mi-shong-i-ni-vi, Shong-a-pa-vi, Te-wa, Wol-pi, and Si-choam-a-vi. The last three are known as the Moqui Towns.

We remained nearly two months in the province, studying the language and customs of the people; and I shall drop the narrative of travel, to describe the towns, the people, and their daily life.

Oraibi and the three Moqui towns are greatly dilapidated, and their original plans are not easily discovered. The other three towns are much better preserved. There are now about two thousand seven hundred inhabitants in the seven towns, probably but

THE HOUSE OF TAL-TI, CHIEF OF THE COUNCIL IN THE TOWN OF ORAIBI.

16

A COVERED PASSAGEWAY OF SHUPAULOVI.

a small proportion of what they at one time contained. The towns are all built on high cliffs or rocks, doubtless for greater security against the common nomadic enemies, the Navajos on the north and Apaches on the south. Each town has a form peculiar to itself and adapted to its site—Shi-pau-a-luv-i the most regular, Oraibi the most irregular. Shi-pau-a-luv-i is built about an open court; the exterior wall is unbroken, so that you enter the town by a covered way. Standing within, the houses are seen to be two, three, and four stories high, built in terraces—that is, the second story is set back upon the first, the third back upon the second, the fourth upon the third; the fourth or upper story being therefore very narrow. Usually, to enter a room on the first story from the court, it is necessary to climb by a ladder to the top of the story, and descend by another through a hatchway. To go up to the third or fourth story you climb by a stairway made in the projecting wall of the partition. The lower rooms are chiefly used for purposes of storage. The main assembly-room is in the second story, sometimes in the third. The rooms below are quite small, eight or ten feet square, and about six feet high. The largest room occupied by a family is often twenty to twenty-four feet long by twelve or fifteen feet wide, and about eight feet between floor and ceiling. Usually all the rooms are carefully plastered, and sometimes painted with rude devices. For doors and windows there are openings only, except that sometimes small windows are glazed with thin sheets of selenite, leaf-like crystals of gypsum.

In a corner of each principal room a little fire-place is seen, large enough to hold about a peck of wood; a stone chimney is built in the corner, and often capped outside with a pottery pipe. The exterior of the house is very irregular and unsightly, and the streets and courts are filthy; but within, great cleanliness is observed. The people are very hospitable and quite ceremonious. Enter a house and you are invited to take a seat on a mat placed for you upon the floor, and some refreshment is offered—perhaps a melon, with a little bread, perhaps peaches or apricots. After you have eaten, every

thing is carefully cleaned away, and, with a little broom made of feathers, the matron or her daughter removes any crumbs or seeds which may have been dropped. They are very economical people; the desolate circumstances under which they live, the distance to the forest and the scarcity of game, together with their fear of the neighboring

MI-SHONG-I-NI-VI.

Navajos and Apaches, which prevents them from making excursions to a distance—all combine to teach them the most rigid economy. Their wood is packed from a distant forest on the backs of mules, and when a fire is kindled but a few small fragments are used, and when no longer needed the brands are extinguished, and the remaining pieces preserved for future use.

Their corn is raised in fields near by, out in the drifting sands, by digging pits eighteen inches to two feet deep, in which the seeds are planted early in the spring, while the ground is yet moist. When it has ripened, it is gathered, brought in from the fields in baskets, carried by the women and stored away in their rooms, being carefully corded. They take great pains to raise corn of different colors, and have the corn of each color stored in a separate room. This is ground by hand to a fine flour in stone mills, then made into a paste like a rather thick gruel.

NORTH KIVAS OF SHUMOPAVI, FROM THE NORTHEAST.

In every house there is a little oven made of a flat stone eighteen or twenty inches square, raised four or five inches from the floor, and beneath this a little fire is built. When the oven is hot and the dough mixed in a little vessel of pottery, the good woman plunges her hand in the mixture and rapidly smears the broad surface of the furnace rock with a thin coating of the paste. In a few moments the film of batter is baked; when taken up it looks like a sheet of paper. This she folds and places on a tray. Having made seven sheets of this paper bread from the batter of one color and placed them on the tray, she takes batter of another color, and, in this way, makes seven sheets of each of the several colors of corn batter.

In this warm and dry climate the people live principally out of doors or on the tops of their houses, and it is a merry sight to see a score or two of little naked children climbing up and down the stairways and ladders, and running about the tops of the houses engaged in some active sport.

In every house vessels of stone and pottery are found in great abundance. These Indian women have great skill in ceramic art, decorating their vessels with picture-writings in various colors, but chiefly black.

In the early history of this country, before the advent of the Spaniard, these people raised cotton, and from it made their clothing; but between the years 1540 and 1600 they were supplied with sheep, and now the

SI-CHOAM-A-VI AND TE-WA.

They have many curious ways of preparing their food, but perhaps the daintiest dish is "virgin hash." This is made by chewing morsels of meat and bread, rolling them in the mouth into little lumps about the size of a horse-chestnut, and then tying them up in bits of corn husk. When a number of these are made, they are thrown into a pot and boiled like dumplings. The most curious thing of all is, that only certain persons are allowed to prepare these dumplings; the tongue and palate kneading must be done by a virgin. An old feud is sometimes avenged by pretending hospitality, and giving to the enemy dumplings made by a lewd woman.

greater part of their clothing is made of wool, though all their priestly habiliments, their wedding and burying garments, are still made of cotton.

Men wear moccasins, leggings, shirts and blankets; the women, moccasins with long tops, short petticoats dyed black, sometimes with a red border below, and a small blanket or shawl thrown over the body so as to pass over the right shoulder under the left arm. A long girdle of many bright colors is wound around the waist. The outer garment is also black. The women have beautiful, black glossy hair, which is allowed to grow very long, and which they take great pains in dressing. Early in the morn-

THE CHIEF KIVA OF SHUPAULOVI.

H. Hobart Nichols, 90.

21

ing, immediately after breakfast, if the weather is pleasant, the women all repair to the tops of the houses, taking with them little vases of water, and wash, comb, and braid one another's hair. It is washed in a decoction of the soap plant, a species of yucca, and then allowed to dry in the open air. The married ladies have their hair braided and rolled in a knot at the back of the head, but the maidens have it parted along the middle line above, and each lock carefully braided, or twisted and rolled into a coil supported by little wooden pins so as to cover each ear, giving them a very fantastic appearance.

I have already said that the people are hospitable; they are also very polite. If you meet them out in their fields, they salute you with a greeting which seems to mean, " May the birds sing happy songs in your fields." They have many other greetings for special occasions. Do one a favor and he thanks you; if a man, he says, " Kwa kwa;" if a woman, " Es-ka-li." And this leads me to say that there is a very interesting feature in their language found among people of the same grade of civilization in other parts of the world: many words are used exclusively by men, others by women. " Father," as spoken by a girl, is one word; spoken by a boy it is another; and nothing is considered more vulgar among these people than for a man to use a woman's word, or a woman a man's.

At the dawn of day the governor of the town goes up to the top of his house and calls on the people to come forth. In a few moments the upper story of the town is covered with men, women, and children. For a few minutes he harangues them on the duties of the day. Then, as the sun is about to rise, they all sit down, draw their blankets over their heads and peer out through a little opening and watch for the sun. As the upper limb appears above the horizon every person murmurs a prayer, and continues until the whole disk is seen, when the prayer ends and the people turn to their various avocations. The young men gather

SCENE IN TE-WA.

in the court about the deep fountain stripped naked, except that each one has a belt to which are attached bones, hoofs, horns, or metallic bells, which they have been able to procure from white men. These they lay aside for a moment, plunge into the water, step out, tie on their belts, and dart away on their morning races over the rocks, running as if for dear life. Then the old men collect the little boys, sometimes with little whips, and compel them to go through the same exercises. When the athletes return, each family gathers in the large room for breakfast. This over, the women ascend to the tops of their houses to dress, and the men depart to the fields or woods, or gather in the kiva to chat or weave.

This kiva, as it is called in their own tongue, is called "*Estufa*" by the Spaniards, and is spoken of by writers in English as the " Sweat House." It is, in fact, an underground compartment, chiefly intended for religious ceremonies, but also used as a place of social resort. A deep pit is exca-

A Tusayan field shelter

Grinding stones in a Hopi house

23

vated in the shaly rock and covered with long logs, over which are placed long reeds, these, in turn, covered with earth, heaped in a mound above. A hole, or hatchway, is left, and the entrance to the kiva is by a thunder, and a god of rain, the sun, the moon, and the stars; and, in addition, each town has its patron deity. There seems, also, to be engrafted on their religion a branch of ancestral worship. Their notion

PRAYING FOR RAIN.

ladder down the hatchway. The walls are plastered, little niches, or quadrangular recesses, being left, in which are kept the paraphernalia of their religious ceremonies. At the foot of the wall, there is a step, or bench, which is used as a seat. When the people assemble in the kiva, a little fire is built immediately under the hatchway, which forms a place of escape for the smoke. Here the elders assemble for council, and here their chief religious ceremonies are performed, for the people are remarkable for their piety. Some of these ceremonies are very elaborate and long. I witnessed one which required twenty-four hours for its performance. The people seem to worship a great number of gods, many of whom are personified objects, powers and phenomena of nature. They worship a god of the north, and a god of the south; a god of the east, and a god of the west; a god of of the form and constitution of the world is architectural; that it is composed of many stories. We live in the second. Ma-chi-ta, literally the leader, probably an ancestral god, is said to have brought them up from the lower story to the next higher, in which we now live. The heaven above is the ceiling of this story, the floor of the next. Their account of their rescue from the lower world by Ma-chi-ta is briefly as follows: The people below were a medley mass of good and bad, and Ma-chi-ta determined to rescue the former, and leave the latter behind. So he called to his friends to bring him a young tree, and, looking overhead at the sky of that lower world, the floor of this, he discovered a crack, and placed the young and growing tree immediately under it. Then he raised his hands and prayed, as did all his followers; and, as he prayed, the tree grew, until its branches were thrust through

24

A COVERED PASSAGEWAY IN MASHONGNAVI.

the crevice in the lower-world sky. Then the people climbed up, in one long stream; still up they came until all the good were there. Ma-chi-ta, standing on the brink of the crevice, looked down, and saw the tree filled with the bad, who were following; then he caught the growing ladder by the upper boughs, twisted it from its foundation

"Bring me seven virgins;" and they brought him seven virgins. And he taught the virgins to weave a wonderful fabric, which he held aloft, and the breeze carried it away to the sky; and behold! it was transformed into a full-orbed moon. The same breeze also carried the flocculent fragments of cotton to the sky, and lo! these took the shape

RUINS ON THE BRINK OF GLEN CAÑON.

in the soil beneath, and threw it over, and the wicked fell down in a pile of mangled, groaning, cursing humanity. When the people had spread out through this world, they found the ceiling, or sky, so low that they could not walk without stooping, and they murmured. Then Ma-chi-ta, standing in the very center of this story, placed his shoulder against the sky, and lifted it to where it now is.

Still it was cold and dark, and the people murmured and cursed Ma-chi-ta, and he said: "Why do you complain? Bring me seven baskets of cotton;" and they brought him seven baskets of cotton. And he said:

of bright stars. And still it was cold; and again the people murmured, and Ma-chi-ta chided them once more, and said, "Bring me seven buffalo robes;" and they brought him seven buffalo robes. "Send me seven strong, pure young men;" and they sent him seven young men, whom he taught to weave a wonderful fabric of the buffalo fur. And when it was done, he held it aloft, and a whirlwind carried it away to the sky, where it was transformed into the sun.

I have given but a very bare account of these two chapters in their unwritten bible—the bringing up of the people from the lower world to this, and the creation of

BACK WALL OF A MASHONGNAVI HOUSE ROW.

the heavenly bodies. As told by them, there are many wonderful incidents; the travels, the wandering, the wars, the confusion of tongues, the dispersion of the people into tribes — all these are given with much circumstance.

Mu-ing-wa is the god of rain, and the ceremony of which I have made mention as lasting twenty-four hours was in honor of this god, immediately after the gathering of the harvest. A priest from Oraibi, one from Shi-pau-i-luv-i, one from Shong-a-pa-vi, together with the one from Mi-shong-i-ni-vi, gathered in the kiva at this latter place. An old woman, a grandmother, her daughter, a mother and her granddaughter, a virgin, three women in the same ancestral line, were also taken into the kiva, where I was permitted to join them. Before this I had known of many ceremonies being performed, but they had always refused me admittance,

WATCH-TOWER AT McELMO CAÑON.

and it was only the day before, at a general council held at Oraibi, that it was decided to admit me. The men were entirely naked, except that during certain parts of the ceremony they wrapped themselves in blankets,

and a blanket was furnished me at such times for the same purpose. The three women were naked, except that each had a cincture made of pure white cotton wound about the loins and decorated with tassels. Event followed event, ceremony ceremony so rapidly during the twenty-four hours, that I was not able on coming out to write a very definite account of the sacred rites, but I managed to carry away with me some things which I was afterward able to record in my notes from time to time.

I have said that the ceremony was in honor of Mu-ing-wa, the god of rain. It was a general thanksgiving for an abundant harvest, and a prayer for rain during the coming season. Against one end of the kiva was placed a series of picture writings on wooden tablets. Carved wooden birds on little wooden pedestals, and many pitchers and vases, were placed about the room. In the niches were kept the collection of sacred jewels—little crystals of quartz, crystals of calcite, garnets, beautiful pieces of jasper, and other bright or fantastically shaped stones, which, it was claimed, they had kept for many generations. Corn, meal, flour, white and black sand were used in the ceremony at different times. There were many sprinklings of water, which had been previously consecrated by ceremony and prayer. Often the sand or meal was scattered about. Occasionally during the twenty-four hours a chorus of women singers was brought into the kiva, and the general ceremony was varied by dancing and singing. The dancing was performed by single persons or by couples, or by a whole bevy of women; but the singing was always in chorus, except a kind of chant from time to time by the elder of the priests. My knowledge of the language was slight, and I was able to comprehend but little of what was said; but I think I obtained, by questioning and close observation, and gathering a few words here and there, some general idea of what they were doing. About every two hours there was a pause in the ceremony, when refreshments were brought in, and twenty minutes or half an hour was given to general conversation, and I always took advantage of such a time to have the immediately preceding ceremony explained to me as far as possible. During one of these resting times I took pains to make a little diagram of the position which had been assumed by the different parties engaged, and to note down, as far as possible, the various performances, which I will endeavor to explain.

A little to one side of the fire (which was in the middle of the chamber) and near the sacred paintings, the four priests took their positions in the angles of a somewhat regular quadrilateral. Then the virgin placed a large vase in the middle of the space; then she brought a pitcher of water, and, with a prayer, the old man poured a quantity into the vase. The same was done in turn by the other priests. Then the maiden brought on a little tray or salver, a box or pottery case containing the sacred jewels, and, after a prayer, the old man placed some of these jewels in the water, and the same ceremony was performed by each of the other priests. Whatever was done by the old priest was also done by the others in succession. Then the maiden brought kernels of corn on a tray, and these were in like manner placed on the water. She then placed a little brush near each of the priests. These brushes were made of the feathers of the beautiful warblers and humming-birds found in that region. Then she placed a tray of meal near each of the priests, and a tray

AN-TI-NAINTS, PU-TU-SU, AND WI-CHUTS (POSY, EYELASH, AND BIRDIE.)

of white sand, and a tray of red sand, and a tray of black sand. She then took from the niche in the wall a little stone vessel, in which had been ground some dried leaves, and placed it in the center of the space between the men. Then on a little willow-ware tray, woven of many-colored strands, she brought four pipes of the ancient pattern—hollow cones, in the apex of which were inserted the stems. Each of the priests filled his pipe with the ground leaves from the stone vessel. The maiden lighted a small fantastically painted stick and gave it to the priest, who lighted his pipe and smoked it with great vigor, swallowing the smoke, until it appeared that his stomach and mouth were distended. Then, kneeling over the vase, he poured the smoke from his mouth

into it, until it was filled, and the smoke piled over and gradually rose above him, forming a cloud. Then the old man, taking one of the little feather brushes, dipped it into the vase of water and sprinkled the floor of the kiva, and, standing up, clasped his hands, turned his face upward, and prayed. "Mu-ing-wa! very good; thou dost love us, for thou didst bring us up from the lower world. Thou didst teach our fathers, and their wisdom has descended to us. We eat no stolen bread. No stolen sheep are found in our flocks. Our young men ride not the stolen ass. We beseech thee, Mu-ing-wa, that thou wouldst dip thy brush, made of the feathers of the birds of heaven, into the lakes of the skies, and scatter water over the earth, even as I scatter water over the floor of this kiva; Mu-ing-wa, very good."

Then the white sand was scattered over the floor, and the old man prayed that during the coming season Mu-ing-wa would

29

break the ice in the lakes of heaven, and grind it into ice dust (snow) and scatter it over the land, so that during the coming winter the ground might be prepared for the planting of another crop. Then, after

RUINS AT THE HEAD OF JUGELMO CAÑON

another ceremony with kernels of corn, he prayed that the corn might be impregnated with the life of the water, and made to bring forth an abundant harvest. After a ceremony with the jewels, he prayed that the

corn might ripen, and that each kernel might be as hard as one of the jewels. Then this part of the ceremony ceased. The vases, and pitchers, and jewels, and other paraphernalia of the ceremony were placed away in the niche by the mother.

At day-break on the second morning, when the ceremonies had ceased, twenty-five or thirty maidens came down into the kiva, disrobed themselves, and were re-clothed in gala dress, variously decorated with feathers and bells, each assisting the other. Then their faces were painted by the men in this wise : A man would take some paint in his mouth, thoroughly mix it with saliva, and with his finger paint the girl's face with one color, in such manner as seemed right to him, and she was then turned over to another man who had another color prepared. In this way their faces were painted yellow, red, and blue. When all was ready, a line was formed in the kiva, at the head of which was the grandmother, and at the foot the virgin priestess, who had attended through the entire ceremony. As soon as the line was formed below, the men, with myself, having in the meantime reclothed ourselves, went up into the court and were stationed on the top of the house nearest the entrance to the kiva. We found all the people of this village, and what seemed to me all the people of the surrounding villages, assembled on top of the houses, men, women, and children, all standing expectant.

As the procession emerged from the kiva by the ladder, the old woman commenced to chant. Slowly the procession marched about the court and around two or three times, and then to the center, where the maidens formed a circle, the young virgin priestess standing in the center. She held in her hand a beautifully wrought willow-work tray, and all the young men stood on the brink of the wall next to the plaza, as if awaiting a signal. Then the maiden, with eyes bandaged, turned round and round, chanting something which I could not understand, until she should be thoroughly confused as to the direction in which the young men stood. Then she threw out of the circle in which she stood the tray which she held, and, at that instant, every young athlete sprang from the wall and rushed toward the tray and entered into the general conflict to see who should obtain it. No blows were given, but they caught each other about the waist and around the neck,

HOUSES BUILT OVER IRREGULAR SITES, WALPI.

31

tumbling and rolling about into the court until, at last, one got the tray into his possession for an instant, threw it aloft and was declared the winner. With great pride he carried it away. Then the women returned to the kiva. In a few minutes afterward

ANCIENT CLIFF HOUSE

they emerged again, another woman carrying a tray, and so the contests were kept up until each maiden had thrown a tray into the court-yard, and it had been won by some of the athletes. About ten o'clock these contests ended, and the people retired to their homes, each family in the village inviting its friends from the surrounding villages, and for an hour there was feasting and revelry. During the afternoon there were races, and afterward dancing, which was continued until midnight.

In a former article I have briefly described the system of picture-writings found in use among these people. These are rude etchings on the rocks or paintings on tablets of wood. They are simply mnemonic, and are, of course, without dates. A great buffalo hunt is recorded with a picture of a man standing in front of and pointing an arrow at one of these animals. The record of a great journey is made with a rude map. On the cliff near Oraibi, I found a record like this etched on a stone. Below and to the left were three Spaniards, the leader with a sword, the two followers carrying spears. Above and to the right were three natives in an attitude of rolling rocks. Near by was a Spaniard prone on the ground, with a native pouring water on his head. Tal-ti, whose name means "peep of day," because he was born at dawn, explained to me that the record was made by their ancestors a very long time ago, and that the explanation had been handed down as follows : Their town was attacked by the Spaniards ; the commander was a gallant fellow, who attempted to lead his men up the stone stairway to the town, but the besieged drove them back with rolling stones, and the Spanish captain was wounded and left by his followers. The people, in admiration of his valor, took him to a spring near by, poured water on him and, dressed his wounds and, when they were healed, permitted him to return.

Tal-ti's description of the scene was quite vivid, and even dramatic, especially when he described the charge of the Spaniards rushing forward and shouting their war cries, "*Santiago ! Santiago ! Santiago !*"

Thus in this desert land we find an agricultural people; a people living in stone houses, with walls laid in mortar and plastered within, houses two, three, four, five, or

AN INDIAN HUNTER.

six stories high; a people having skill in the manufacture and ornamentation of pottery, raising cotton, and weaving and dyeing their own clothing, skilled in a system of picture-writings, having a vast store of mythology, and an elaborate, ceremonious religion; without beasts of burden, and having no knowledge of metals, all their tools being made of bones, stone, or wood. Such was their condition when found by the first Europeans who invaded their lands. Early in the recorded history of this country they obtained from the Spaniards a few tools of iron, some sheep, which they raised for their flesh as well as for their wool, and asses, which they use as a means of transportation.

The seven hamlets of this province form only one of many groups discovered by those early Spanish adventurers. Altogether, about sixty towns were found by them; about

half of these were destroyed, and, in all the remaining towns, except the seven, a new religion was imposed upon the people. It should rather be said that Christian forms and Christian ideas were ingrafted on the old pagan stock. Most of the towns outside of this province are watched over by Catholic priests, and the pagan rites and ceremonies are prohibited. But occasionally the people steal away from their homes and assemble on the mountains or join the people of the " Province of Tusayan " in the kivas, and celebrate the rites of their ancient religion.

" Who are these people ? " is a question often asked. Are they a remnant of some ancient invading race from the Eastern Continent ? I think not. Linguistic evidence shows them to be nearly related to some of the nomadic tribes of the Rocky Mountains, such as the Shoshones, Utes, Pai Utes, and Comanches. The region of country between the Rocky Mountains and the Sierras, stretching from northern Oregon to the Gulf of California, is occupied by many tribes speaking languages akin to one another. These town-building people seem to be a branch of this great family; now, but a remnant of this branch is left; but there was a time when they were a vast people. The ruins of these towns are found in great profusion throughout Nevada, Utah, Colorado, New Mexico, Arizona, and Southern California. On every stream, and at almost every spring of importance, vestiges of this race may be found. Where Salt Lake City now stands, in that ancient time there stood a settlement of the people calling themselves Shi-nu-mos, a word signifying " We, the wise." I have visited nearly every settlement in the Territory of Utah, and many in the State of Nevada, and have never failed, on examination, to find evidences of an ancient town on the same site, or one near by. On the eastern slope of the Rocky Mountains they have also been found; one near Golden City by Captain Berthoud, and many others on the same slope to the southward. I have found them on the western slope of the same system of mountains, on the Yampa, White and Grand Rivers; and

Dr. Newberry and Mr. Jackson have found them in great abundance on the San Juan and its tributaries. The history of the exploration of New Mexico and Arizona is replete with accounts of these vestiges of ancient life.

Over all this vast territory, in every beautiful valley and glen, by every stream of water and every spring, on the high mountains, on the cliffs, away out in the deserts of drifting sand, and down in the deep cañon gorges by which much of the country is traversed—everywhere are found ruins, stone implements or fragments of pottery.

How have these people been so nearly destroyed? From a somewhat careful examination of the facts at hand, I have an explanation to offer, though I cannot here give the fragments of evidence on which it rests. There are two great bodies of Indians in this country who are intruders—the Navajos and Apaches, and a number of small tribes in California who speak Athabascan languages, and who originally dwelt far to the north in British America. The Pueblo people call them their northern enemies. It seems that these people gradually spread to the south, attracted perhaps by the wealth accumulated by an agricultural and economic people; and, as they swept southward, from time to time, in bold excursions, town after town, and hamlet after hamlet was destroyed; the people were driven into the cañons and among the cliffs, and on the advent of the white man to this continent, only the sixty towns which I have mentioned remained. Of these, there are now but thirty. Of the former inhabitants of the thirty destroyed since the first invasion of the country by the Spaniards, some, at least, have become nomadic, for the Co-a-ni-nis and Wal-la-pais, who now live in the rocks and deep gorges of the San Francisco Plateau, claim that at one time they dwelt in pueblos, near where Zunia now stands.

Interested as we were in this strange people, time passed rapidly, and our visit among them was all too short; but, at last, the time came for us to leave. When we were ready to start we were joined by a small delegation of the Indians, who proposed to travel with us for a few days.

We made our way to Fort Defiance, thence to Fort Wingate, and still on to the East until we reached the Valley of the Rio Grande del Norte. Here we stopped for a day to visit the ancient town of Jemez, and then proceeded to Santa Fé, where our long journey on horseback ended.

View of Walpi on First Mesa

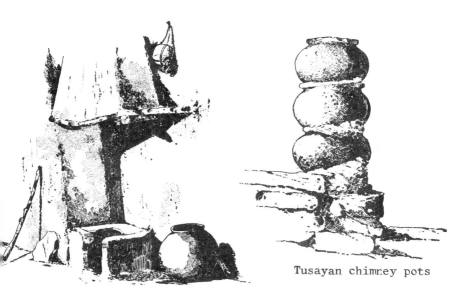

Tusayan chimney pots

Fireplace and chimney hood
at Mishongnovi

A Tusayan notched doorway

An old Hopi notch
log stairway

Fireplace with mantel at Sichomovi

Stone steps and chimney at Oraibi